My Life as a
PIONEER

By Lynda Arnéz

Please visit our website, www.garethstevens.com. For a free color catalog of all our high-quality books, call toll free 1-800-542-2595 or fax 1-877-542-2596.

Library of Congress Cataloging-in-Publication Data

Arnéz, Lynda.
  My life as a pioneer / Lynda Arnéz.
    pages cm — (My place in history)
  Includes index.
ISBN 978-1-4824-3988-5 (pbk.)
ISBN 978-1-4824-3989-2 (6 pack)
ISBN 978-1-4824-3990-8 (library binding)
1. Pioneers—West (U.S.)—Juvenile literature. 2. Frontier and pioneer life—West (U.S.)—Juvenile literature. 3. West (U.S.)—Social life and customs—Juvenile literature. I. Title.
  F596.A717 2016
  978'.02—dc23

                          2015021630

First Edition

Published in 2016 by
Gareth Stevens Publishing
111 East 14th Street, Suite 349
New York, NY 10003

Copyright © 2016 Gareth Stevens Publishing

Designer: Laura Bowen
Editor: Kristen Nelson

Photo credits: Cover, pp. 1, 9 (main), 17 (main) Everett Historical/Shutterstock.com; cover, pp. 1–24 (torn strip) barbaliss/Shutterstock.com; cover, pp. 1–24 (photo frame) Davor Ratkovic/Shutterstock.com; cover, pp. 1–24 (white paper) HABRDA/Shutterstock.com; cover, pp. 1–24 (parchment) M. Unal Ozmen/Shutterstock.com; cover, pp. 1–24 (textured edge) saki80/Shutterstock.com; cover (background) Natalia Sheinkin/Shutterstock.com; pp. 1–24 (paper background) Kostenko Maxim/Shutterstock.com; pp. 5 (main), 9 (inset) Hulton Archive/Getty Images; p. 5 (inset) Sue Smith/Shutterstock.com; p. 7 (main) Mario Geo/Toronto Star/Getty Images; p. 7 (inset) Lori Sparkia/Shutterstock.com; p. 11 (main) MPI/Archive Photos/Getty Images; p. 11 (inset) V. J. Matthew/Shutterstock.com; p. 13 bergserg/Shutterstock.com; p. 15 PhotoQuest/Archive Photos/Getty Images; p. 17 (letter) Gwillhickers/Wikimedia Commons; p. 17 (stamps) BFolkman/Wikimedia Commons; p. 19 (main) Kean Collection/Archive Photos/Getty Images; p. 19 (inset) Sean Pavone/Shutterstock.com; p. 20 DinahRoseH/Wikimedia Commons.

Printed in the United States of America

CPSIA compliance information: Batch #CW16GS: For further information contact Gareth Stevens, New York, New York at 1-800-542-2595.

CONTENTS

Words in the glossary appear in **bold** type the first time they are used in the text.

making a NEW HOME

September 5, 1866

    Today is my birthday! My older brother and sister gave me this little diary because they know I like to write in school so much. I'm going to write down all the important things that happen.

    We're spending most of the day working on our house. We rode in a wagon from Massachusetts to Nebraska Territory more than 2 years ago. We've been living in a house made of **sod** and working on building our **permanent** house since!

Notes from History

The Homestead Act of 1862 encouraged people to head west and settle on the American **frontier**. They were given 160 acres (65 ha) if they agreed to farm it for 5 years.

SOD HOUSE

The US settlers who headed west during the 1800s are called pioneers, since they were the first to move to the new area.

5

school DAYS

October 10, 1866

I'm so happy school started again! I like our schoolhouse's big room, and our teacher, Miss Hopkins, is so nice. She went to a teacher college back east!

I'm very good at reading and writing, and Miss Hopkins has me do the same work as my sister—even though she's 3 years older than me! I'm trying to **memorize** as many words as I can so I can win the spelling bee. Miss Hopkins says I need to work on my handwriting, though.

Notes from History

Pioneer children either walked or rode on horseback to get to school every day.

Schools on the frontier often had only one room for all schoolchildren, no matter what grade they were in.

A Teacher's VISIT

December 17, 1866

Miss Hopkins is staying at our house! Before we go to school in the morning, I feed and milk our cows and get water from the well. I have to do it before the sun rises this time of year! Today, Miss Hopkins came out to help me. It was nice to have another person carry some of the water.

Miss Hopkins helped my mother make dinner, too. I stirred the stew, made with **venison** my father caught earlier this winter.

Notes from History

Teachers on the frontier might live at a schoolhouse, if there was room. More often, they "boarded round," or stayed with a different family for a week or month at a time.

Pioneer children had many tasks to do, including caring for animals and gathering firewood.

Kind NEIGHBORS

February 1, 1867

Our morning didn't start well. Our fire went out! My mother sent my sister and me to our neighbors' house about a mile away for a pan of coals to restart our fire. We had to be careful not to get burned!

The Millers were happy to help. They're our closest neighbors. Mr. Miller and my father hunt together. Mrs. Miller and my mother make cheese and candles together. Mrs. Miller taught my mother how to sew ruffles on my pinafore, too!

Notes from History

Pioneer girls dressed like their mothers in long dresses, bonnets, and aprons called pinafores. Boys wore caps, long-sleeved shirts, and short pants called knickers.

Pioneer families often didn't live very close together. They would travel to visit each other, but the visits were mostly about building a barn, making soap, or other group work.

11

STATEHOOD

March 30, 1867

There's been some exciting news! Nebraska Territory, where we live, is now a state just called Nebraska! My brother said we're the 37th state to join the United States of America. He said a lot more people will come to settle here now.

In honor of the new state, my mother says everyone should take a bath tonight. I have to get the water myself, but warming it up to wash will make carrying the heavy buckets worth it.

Notes from History

Pioneer children didn't wash very often because of how much work it was to get a bath ready. **Laundry**, too, took a long time without today's modern machines!

THE GROWING UNITED STATES

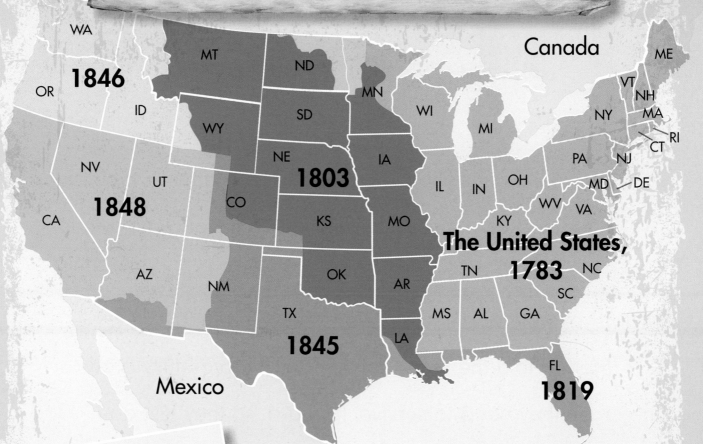

WA

1846

OR

ID

MT

ND

SD

MN

WI

Canada

ME

VT

NH

NY

MA

RI

CT

NV

UT

CO

NE

1803

IA

MI

CA

1848

AZ

NM

KS

MO

OK

AR

TX

1845

LA

Mexico

IL

IN

OH

PA

NJ

MD

DE

KY

WV

VA

The United States, 1783

TN

NC

MS

AL

GA

SC

FL

1819

1867

AK

Alaska

1898

HI

Hawaii

By 1867, almost all the land the present United States covers had been **acquired** by the US government. The Hawaiian Islands weren't part of the United States until 1898.

13

planting TIME

May 3, 1867

My whole family has spent the last few days in the fields. We've planted corn mostly, but my father is trying out a field of wheat this year, too. All last week he was using two of the Millers' oxen in addition to ours to plow the land.

Mother told me many settlers don't successfully grow the crops they need to survive. It's hard, so they just go back to wherever they came from and leave the land for someone else.

Notes from History

Boys and girls worked together on the frontier, unlike in other parts of the country during the 1800s.

Many farming advances came about in the late 1800s. However, most pioneers couldn't afford to buy the new machines that planted and **harvested** crops.

Letter from OUT WEST

June 14, 1867

We got a letter from my Uncle Jim today! He went to California to find gold before I was born and never came back!

My dear family,

I've traveled throughout California these many years. While I've enjoyed its beauty, I haven't found what I was looking for—gold! Now, many are moving into the Rocky Mountains to continue **prospecting***. I, too, will head to Colorado Territory to search for my fortune. First, I wish to come to Nebraska, a closer journey than your home in Massachusetts!*

Jim

Notes from History

When gold was found in California in 1848, many people headed west to make their fortune. Few did, but the discovery caused the population to increase so much that California became a state in 1850!

Some pioneers might only be able to check for mail once every few months if they didn't live near a town.

August 29, 1867

    With the extra help from Uncle Jim, my father said I don't need to help in the fields today! I'm so glad because my mother has been teaching me how to sew. She wants me to help make and repair our family's clothes. I'm practicing by making myself a doll out of old cloth.

    We've been playing "hide the **thimble**" a lot because I've been using mine so much. My sister is always able to find the best hiding spots for it!

Notes from History

Winters could be very cold and hard for pioneers. They made socks and scarves out of wool cloth to keep warm.

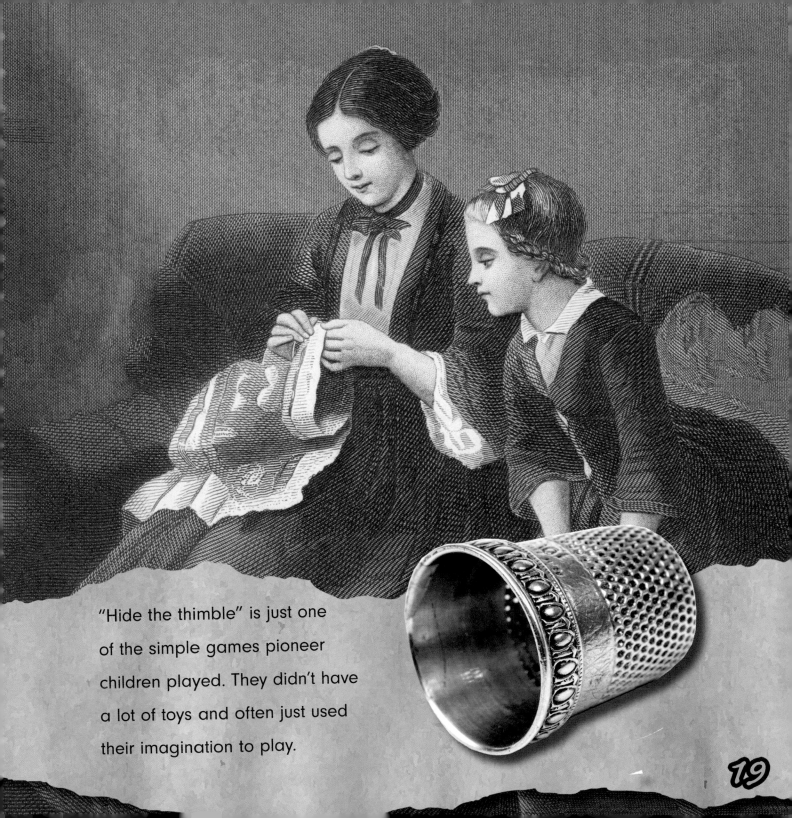

"Hide the thimble" is just one of the simple games pioneer children played. They didn't have a lot of toys and often just used their imagination to play.

Community WORK

September 30, 1867

My mother says it's time to start getting ready for winter. The Millers and a few other families are coming to our house so we can all work together! First, we'll bring in the last of the harvest. Then, we'll store the wheat and corn. The mothers, my sister, and I will start stuffing the **quilts** we've all been working on so they keep everyone's bed nice and warm.

I'm looking forward to dinner the most. When everyone comes over, we make a huge meal!

Quilting bees were a popular way for pioneer women to get together and get some work done!

Play a Pioneer Game!

Anthony-I-Over (Ante Over)

1. Divide into two teams. Have each team stand on one side of a wall, table, or log.

2. The team with the ball is "it." One member calls out "Anthony" and throws the ball to the other team.

3. If the other team doesn't catch the ball, that team is now "it."

4. If the other team catches the ball, both teams have to run to change sides. The team member that caught the ball tries to throw the ball back and hit a player.

5. When a ball hits a player on the other team, that player is out.

6. The first team to get out all the players on the other team wins.

GLOSSARY

acquire: to get as one's own

frontier: a part of a country that has been newly opened for settlement

harvest: to bring in crops. Also, the crops themselves.

laundry: clothes to be washed

memorize: to learn something so well it can be remembered perfectly

permanent: lasting for a long time

prospect: to search an area for valued resources, such as gold

quilt: an often colorful bedcover made from two sheets of cloth and stuffed with wool or cotton

sod: the grass-covered surface of the ground

thimble: a small cap worn on a finger when sewing to protect it from the needle

venison: meat from a deer

For more INFORMATION

Books

Kravitz, Danny. *Surviving the Journey: The Story of the Oregon Trail.* North Mankato, MN: Capstone Press, 2015.

Nolan, Frederick. *Trailblazing the Way West.* Mankato, MN: Black Rabbit Books, 2015.

Onsgard, Bethany. *Life on the Frontier.* Minneapolis, MN: ABDO Publishing, 2015.

Websites

Daily Life on the Frontier
www.ducksters.com/history/westward_expansion/daily_life_on_the_ frontier.php
Find out about the hard life of pioneers on America's frontier.

Kids on the Trail
www.blm.gov/or/oregontrail/education-kids-trail.php
What was the journey to the frontier like for pioneers? Read about it here!

INDEX